Pops 2

Wise Publications
London/New York/Paris/Sydney/
Copenhagen/Madrid

Exclusive Distributors:
Music Sales Limited
8/9 Frith Street, London W1V 5TZ, England.
Music Sales Pty Limited
120 Rothschild Avenue, Rosebery, NSW 2018, Australia.

This book © Copyright 1996 by Wise Publications
Order No. AM936452
ISBN 0-7119-5699-5

Book design by Hutton & Partners
Compiled by Peter Evans
Music arranged by Stephen Duro
Music processed by Allegro Reproductions

Music Sales' complete catalogue lists thousands of titles and is free from your local music shop, or direct from
Music Sales Limited. Please send a cheque/postal order for £1.50 for postage to: Music Sales Limited,
Newmarket Road, Bury St. Edmunds, Suffolk IP33 3YB.

Visit the Internet Music Shop at
http://www.musicsales.co.uk

Your Guarantee of Quality:

Printed in the United Kingdom by
Halstan & Co Limited, Amersham, Buckinghamshire.

A Whole New World
(Aladdin's Theme)
(From Walt Disney's "Aladdin")

Music by Alan Menken
Lyrics by Tim Rice

Moderately

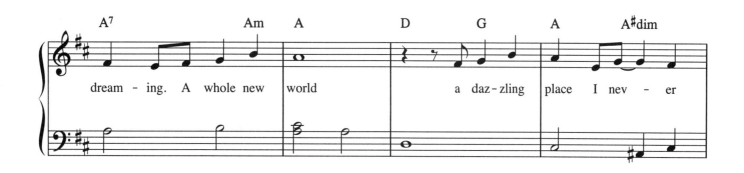

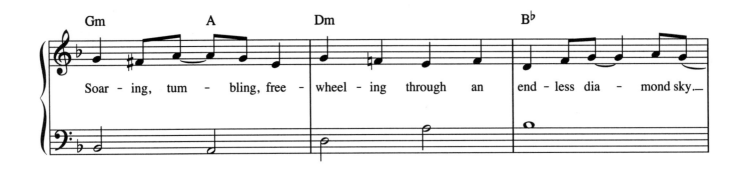

Soar - ing, tum - bling, free - wheel - ing through an end - less dia - mond sky.___

___ A whole new world (Don't you dare close your eyes.)___ a hun - dred

thou - sand things___ to see. I'm like a shoot - ing star. I've

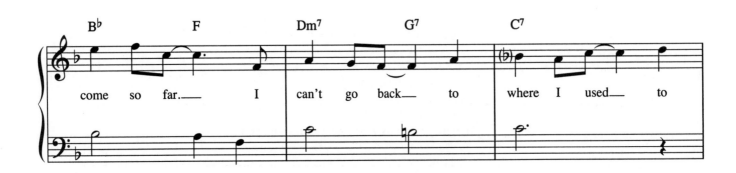

come so far.___ I can't go back___ to where I used___ to

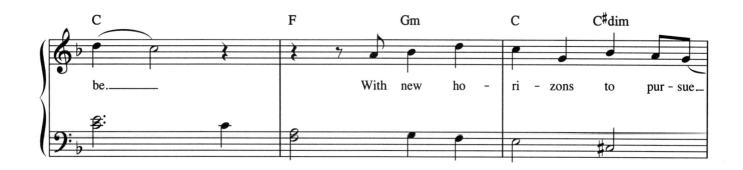

be._____

With new ho - ri - zons to pur - sue_

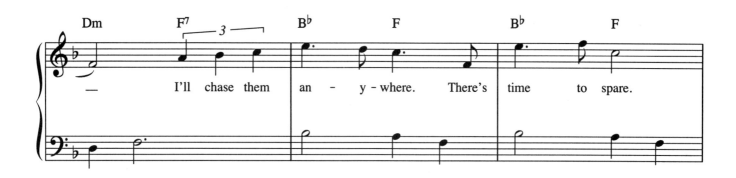

_ I'll chase them an - y - where. There's time to spare.

Let me share_____ this whole new world with you._____

Verse 3:

A whole new world, a whole new world
A new fantastic point of view.
No one to tell us no or where to go
Or say we're only dreaming.
A whole new world with new horizons to pursue.
Ev'ry turn a surprise, ev'ry moment red letter.
I'll chase them anywhere.
There's time to spare.
Anywhere.
There's time to spare.
Let me share this whole new world with you.
A whole new world, that's where we'll be.
A thrilling chase, a wond'rous place for you and me.

I Will Always Love You

Words & Music by Dolly Parton

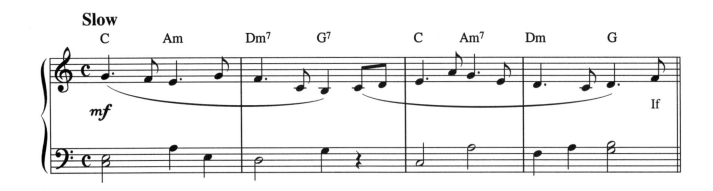

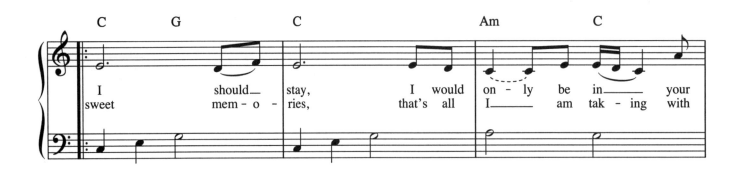

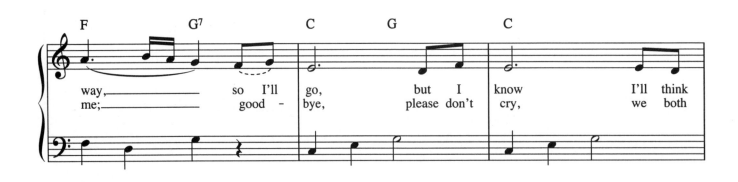

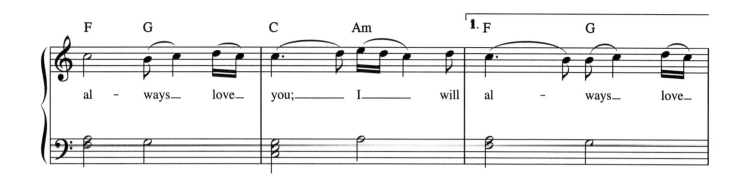

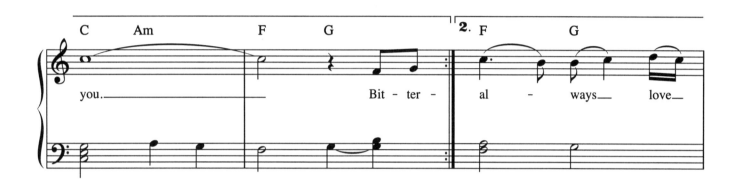

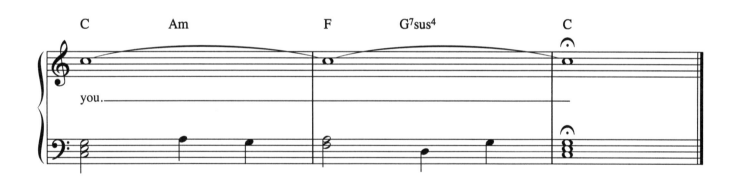

(Recited:)

I hope life treats you kind,
and I hope you have all that you ever dreamed of,
and I wish you joy and happiness,
but above all this, I wish you love.

(Sung:)

And I will always love you,
I will always love you,
I will always love you,
And I will always love you,
I will always love you,
I will always love you.

9

Have I Told You Lately

Words & Music by Van Morrison

Moderately

1,3,5. Have I told you late-ly that I love___ you,___

Have I told you there's no-one___ a-bove___ you___

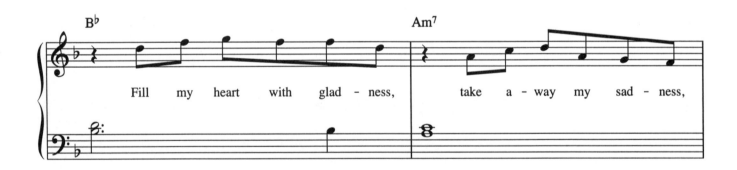

Fill my heart with glad-ness, take a-way my sad-ness,

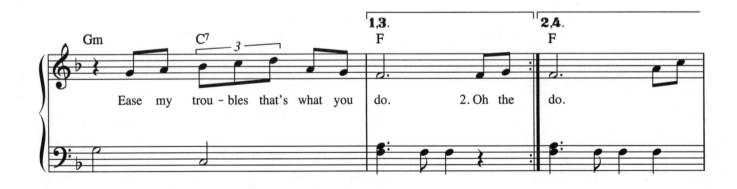

Ease my trou-bles that's what you do. 2. Oh the do.

There's a love that's di-vine And it's yours and it's mine,— like the

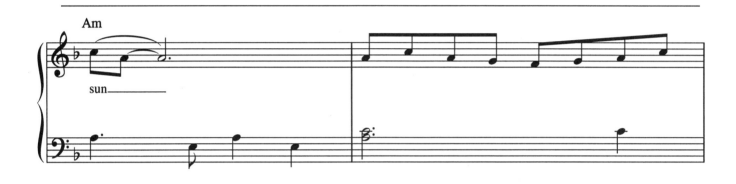

sun

At the end of the day We should give thanks and pray to the

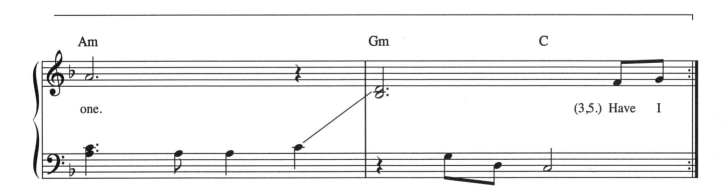

one. (3,5.) Have I

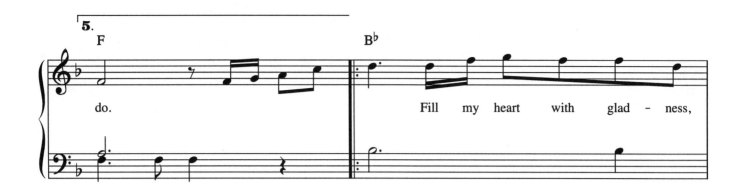

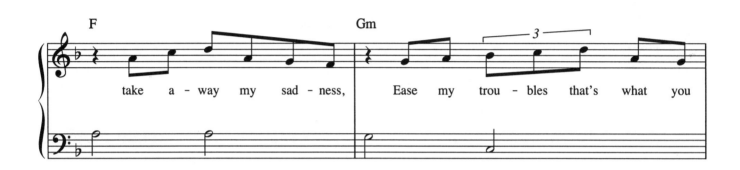

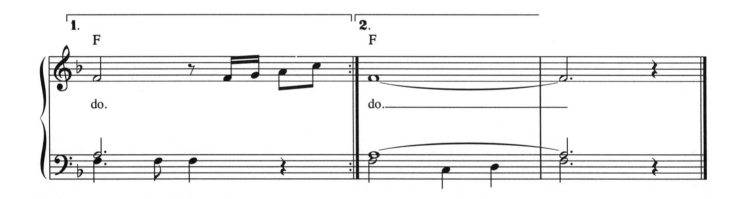

Verse 2:

Oh the morning sun in all its glory
Greets the day with hope and comfort too
And you fill my life with laughter
You can make it better
Ease my troubles that's what you do.

Verse 3: - as Verse 1

Verse 4: - Instrumental

Middle:

There's a love that's divine
And it's yours and its mine
And it shines like the sun
At the end of the day
We will give thanks and pray to the one.

Verse 5: - as Verse 1

Love Is All Around

Words & Music by Reg Presley

Moderately

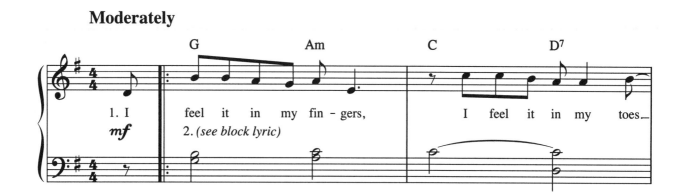

1. I feel it in my fin-gers,
2. *(see block lyric)*
I feel it in my toes.

The love that's all a-round me and so the feel-ing grows.

It's writ-ten on the wind, it's ev-'ry-where I go.

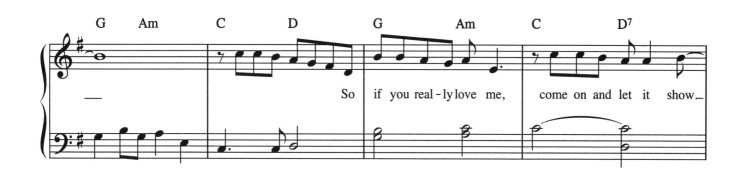

So if you real-ly love me, come on and let it show.

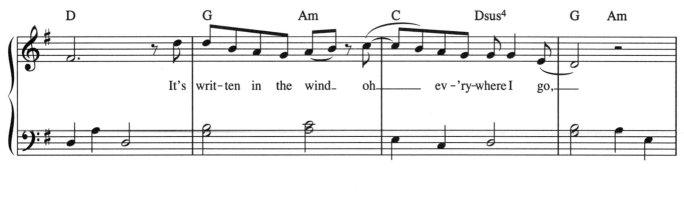

It's | writ-ten in the wind_ oh_ ev-'ry-where I go,_

So | if you real-ly love me, come on and let it

show._ Come on and let it, come on and let_ it,

come on and let_ it, come on and let_ it show._

Verse 2:

I see your face before me
As I lay on my bed;
I cannot get to thinking
Of all the things you said.
You gave your promise to me
And I gave mine to you;
I need someone beside me
In everything I do.

More Than Words

Words & Music by Nuno Bettencourt & Gary Cherone

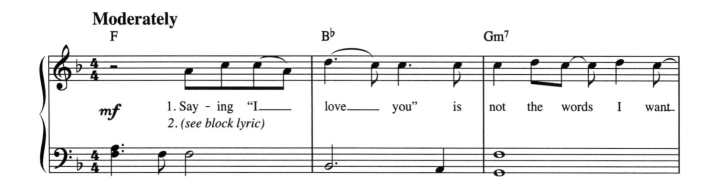

Moderately

1. Say - ing "I____ love____ you" is not the words I want_
2. *(see block lyric)*

_ to_ hear_ from you.___ It's not that I____ want____ you

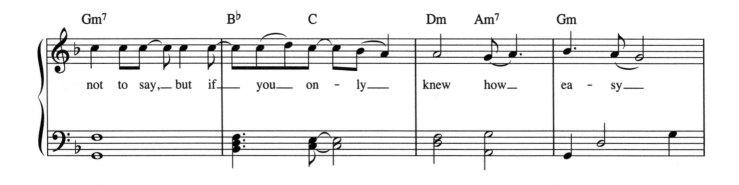

not to say, but if_ you_ on - ly__ knew how_ ea - sy__

it would be_ to_ show me how_ you feel._ More than words____ is

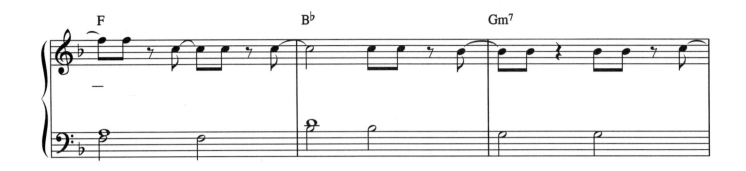

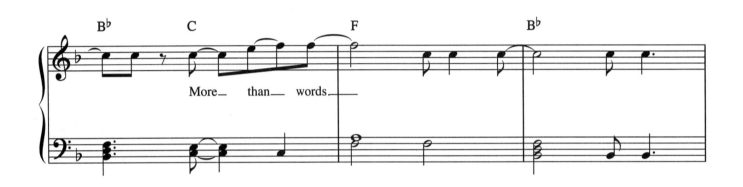

More— than— words—

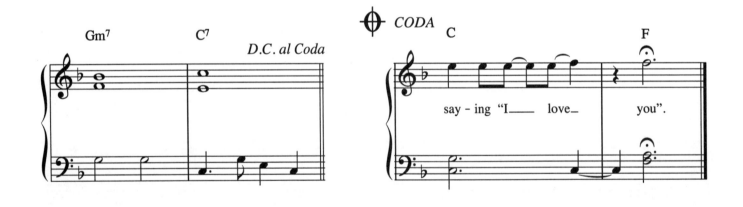

D.C. al Coda

CODA

say - ing "I— love— you".

Verse 2:

Now that I've tried to talk to you
And make you understand
All you have to do is close your eyes
And just reach out your hands
And touch me
Hold me close, don't ever let me go
More than words
Is all I ever needed you to show
Then you wouldn't have to say
That you love me
'Cause I'd already know.

Tears In Heaven

Words & Music by Eric Clapton & Will Jennings

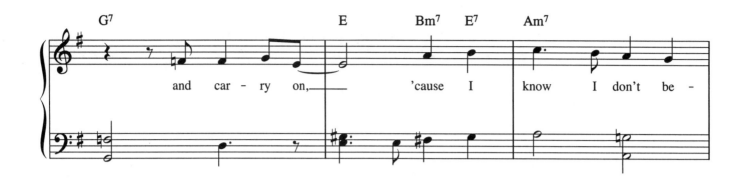

and car - ry on,_____ 'cause I know I don't be -

long_____ here in hea - ven.

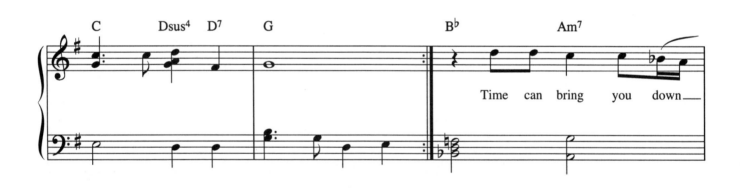

Time can bring you down_____

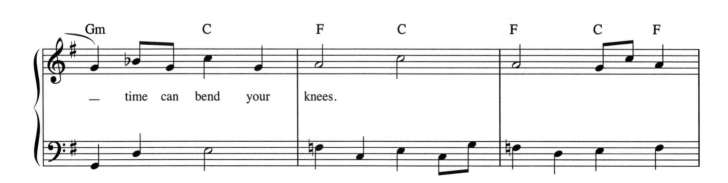

_____ time can bend your knees.

Time can break the heart____ have you beg - ging, please, beg-ging, please.

CODA

ven.

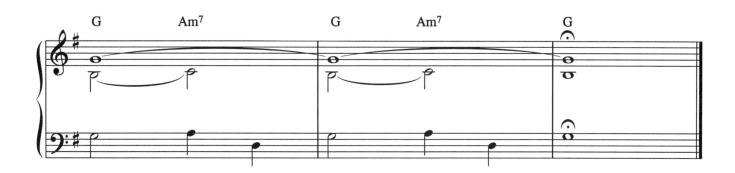

Verse 2:

Would you hold my hand
If I saw you in heaven?
Would you help me stand
If I saw you in heaven?
I'll find my way
Through night and day
'Cause I know I just can't stay
Here in heaven.

Verse 3: (D.S.)

Instrumental solo - 8 bars

Beyond the door
There's peace, I'm sure;
And I know there'll be no more
Tears in heaven.

Verse 4: (D.S.)

Would you know my name
If I saw you in heaven?
Would you be the same
If I saw you in heaven?
I must be strong
And carry on,
'Cause I know I don't belong
Here in heaven.

Run To You

Words & Music by Bryan Adams & Jim Vallance

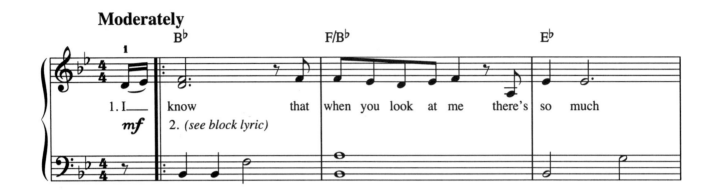

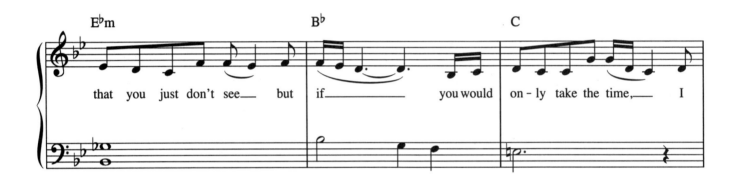

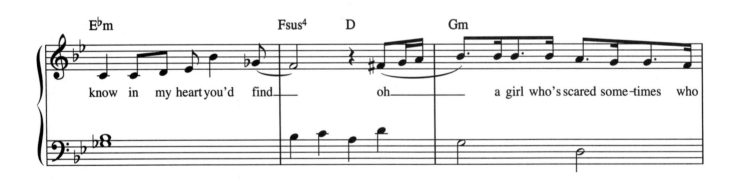

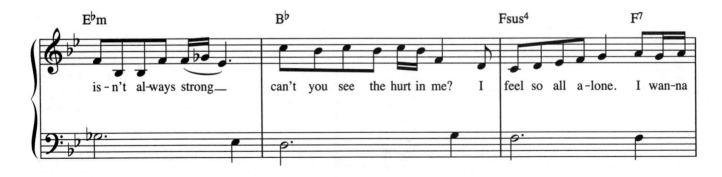

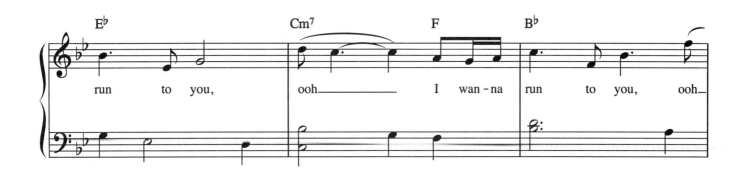

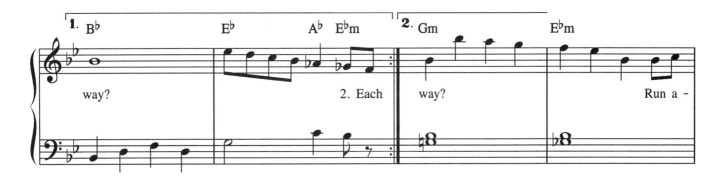

way?___

I need you here, I need you here to

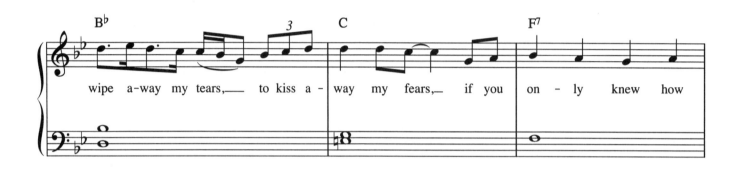

wipe a-way my tears,___ to kiss a - way my fears,___ if you on - ly knew how

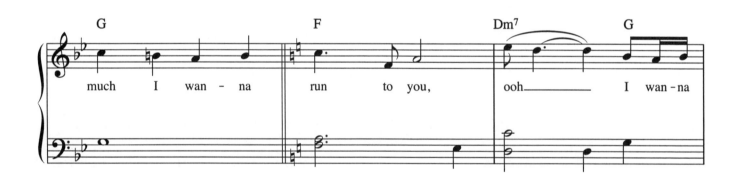

much I wan - na run to you, ooh_____ I wan - na

run to you, ooh_____ won't you hold me in your arms and

24

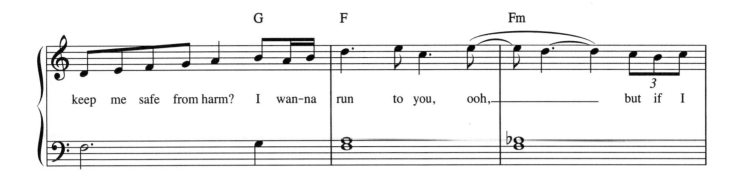

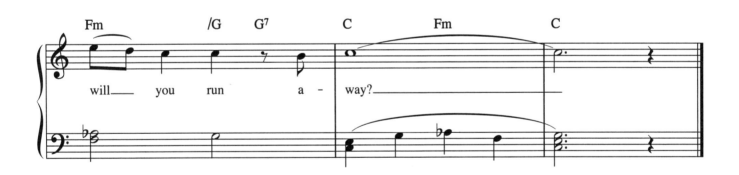

Verse 2:

Each day, each day I play the role of someone
Always in control,
But at night I come home and turn the key,
There's nobody there,
No one cares for me.
Oh, what's the sense of trying hard to find your dreams
Without someone to share them with?
Tell me, what does it mean?

Stay Another Day

Words & Music by Mortimer, Kean & Hawken

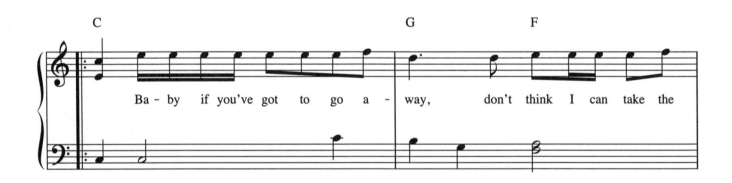

Ba - by if you've got to go a - way, don't think I can take the

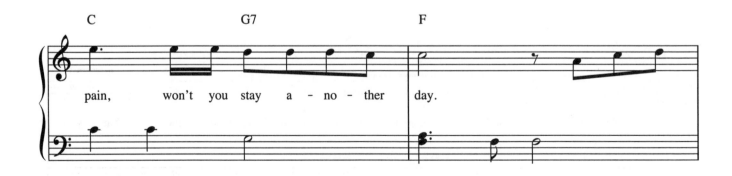

pain, won't you stay a - no - ther day.

Oh don't leave me a - lone like this, don't you say it's the fi - nal

kiss, won't you stay an - oth - er day.

Don't you know we've come too far now, just to
(Verse 2 see block lyric)

go and try to throw it all a - way.

Thought I heard you say you love me, that your

love was gon - na be here__ to stay.

I've on - ly just be - gun to know you, all I can

say is won't you stay just one more day.__

stay.

Ba - by if you've got to go a - way don't think I can take the

28

C   **G7**   **F**

pain   won't you stay an - oth - er   day._____

C   **G**   **F**

Oh don't leave me a - lone like this   don't you say it's the fi - nal

C   **G7**   **1,2.** **F**   **3.** **F**

kiss,   won't you stay an - oth - er   day.   day.

C

Verse 2:

I touch your face while you are sleeping
And hold your hand
Don't understand what's going on
Good times we had return to haunt me
Though it's for you
All that I do seems to be wrong.

Unchain My Heart

Words & Music by Freddy James & Bobby Sharp

Moderately, with a beat

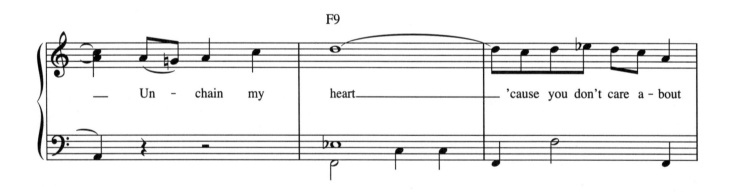

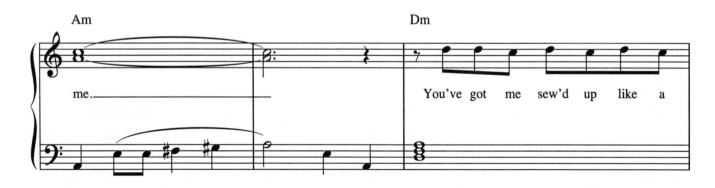

be - fore you drive me in - sane.

Why lead me thro' a life of mi - se - ry ___ when you don't care a bag of

beans for me. ___ Un - chain my heart, oh please, please set me

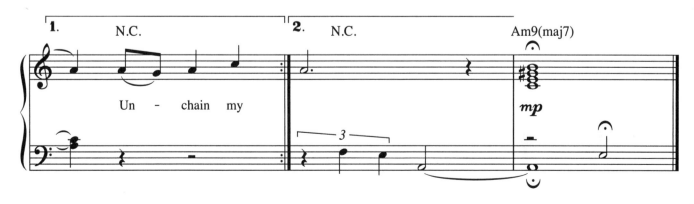

free. *f*   *mf*

1. N.C.   **2.** N.C.   Am9(maj7)

Un - chain my   *mp*

Unchained Melody

Music by Alex North
Words by Hy Zaret

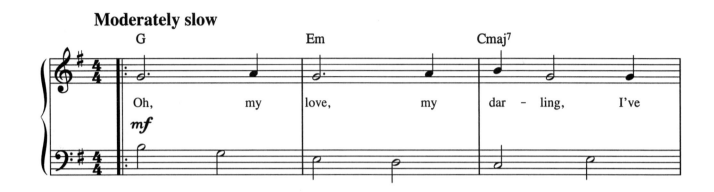

Oh, my love, my dar - ling, I've

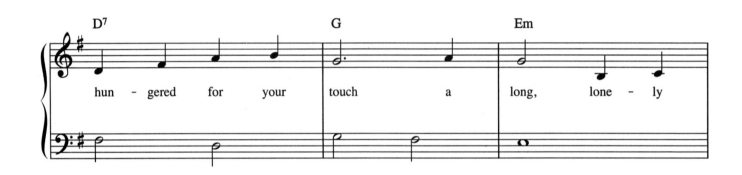

hun - gered for your touch a long, lone - ly

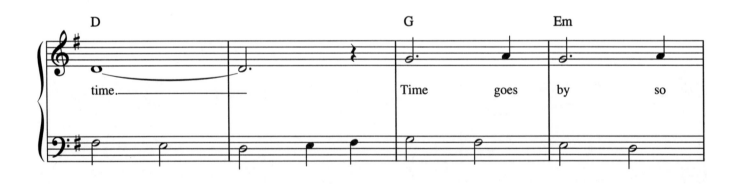

time. Time goes by so

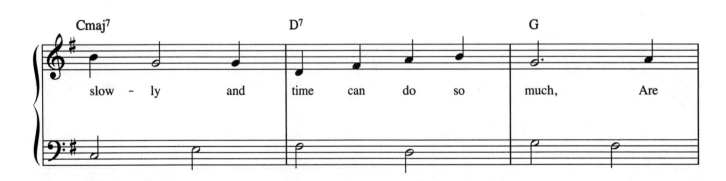

slow - ly and time can do so much, Are

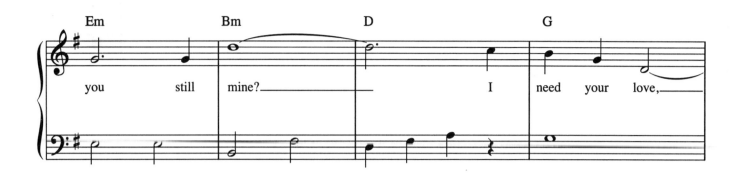

you   still   mine? _____   I   need   your   love, _____

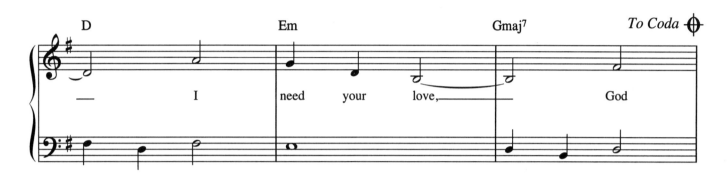

_   I   need   your   love, _____   God

To Coda ⊕

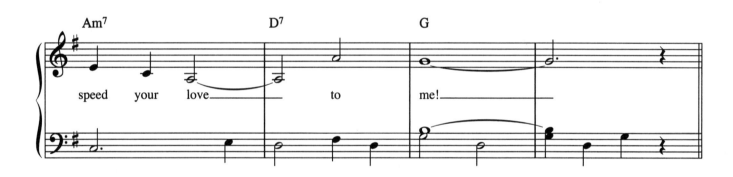

speed   your   love _____   to   me! _____

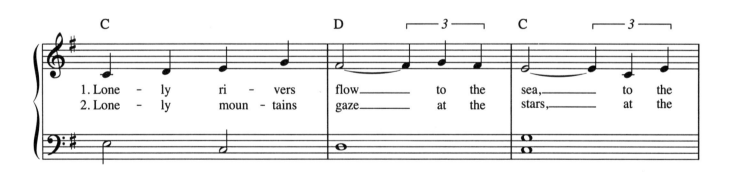

1. Lone - ly   ri - vers   flow _____   to   the   sea, _____   to   the
2. Lone - ly   moun - tains   gaze _____   at   the   stars, _____   at   the

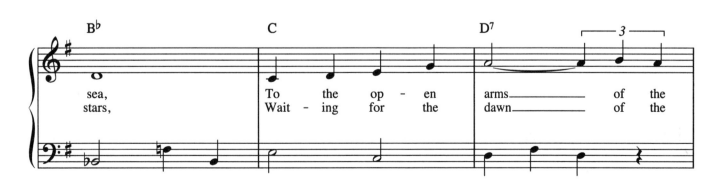

sea,   To   the   op - en   arms _____   of   the
stars,   Wait - ing   for   the   dawn _____   of   the

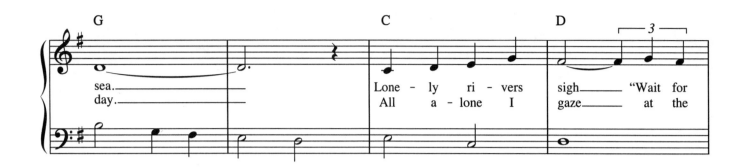

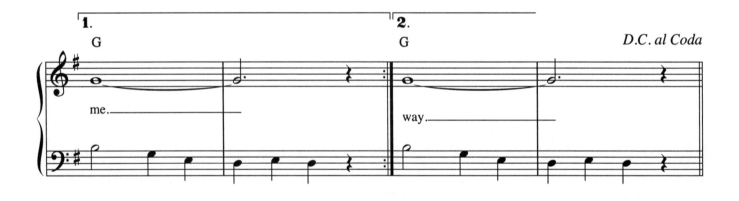

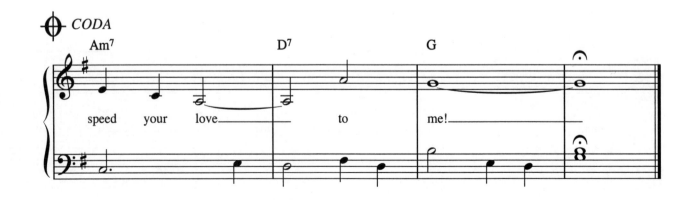

36

Without You

Words & Music by Peter Ham & Tom Evans

Slowly

No, I can't for - get this ev - 'ning or your

face as you were leav - ing, but I guess that's just the way the sto - ry

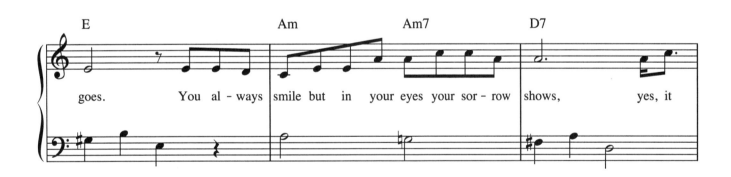

goes. You al - ways smile but in your eyes your sor - row shows, yes, it

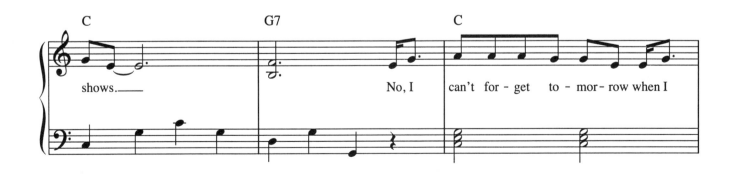

shows.___ No, I can't for - get to - mor - row when I

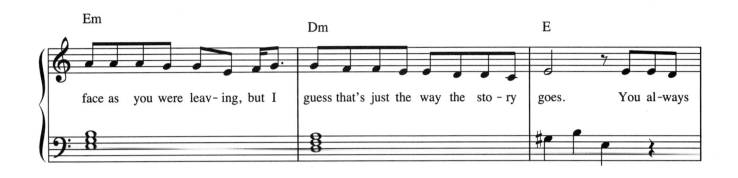

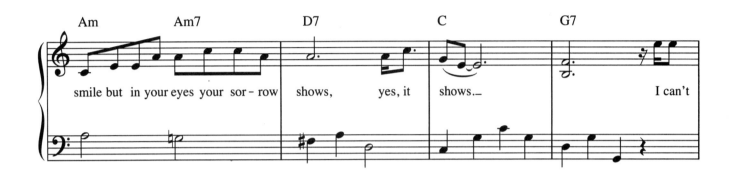

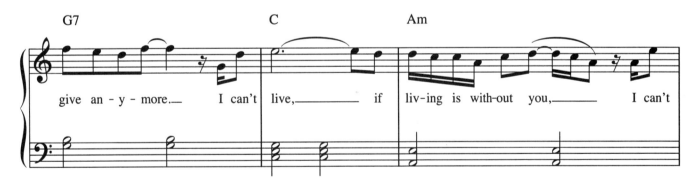

When You Tell Me That You Love Me

Words & Music by Albert Hammond & John Bettis

Moderately

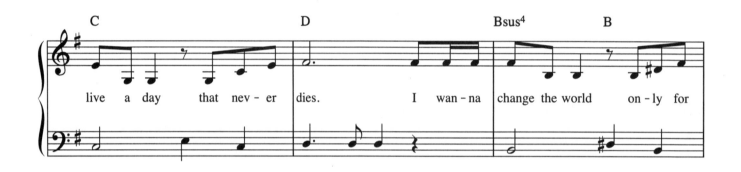

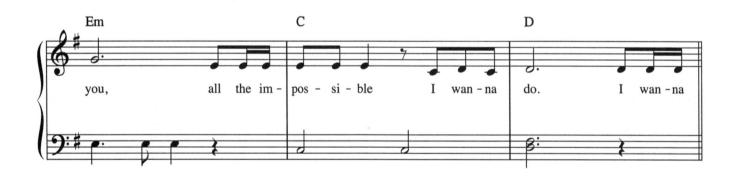

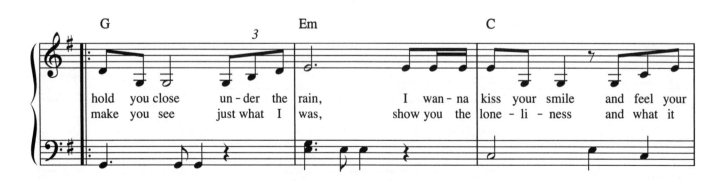

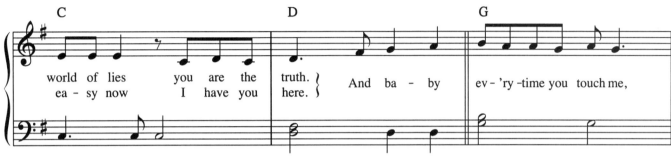

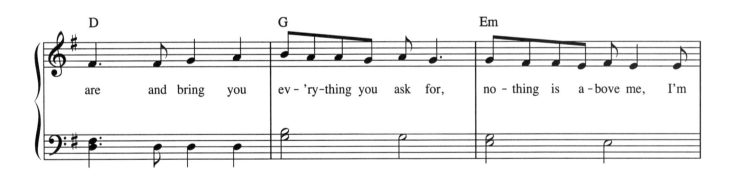

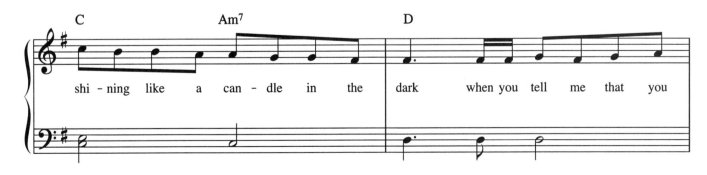

ev-'ry-time you touch me, I be-come a he-ro, I'll make you safe, no mat-ter where you

are. And bring you ev-'ry-thing you ask for, no-thing is a-bove me, I'm

shi-ning like a can-dle in the dark whenyou tell me that you love_____ me.

You love_____ me, when you tell me that you

love_____ me._____

You Are Not Alone

Words & Music by Robert Kelly

way, I am here to stay, but you are not a - lone, but I am here with

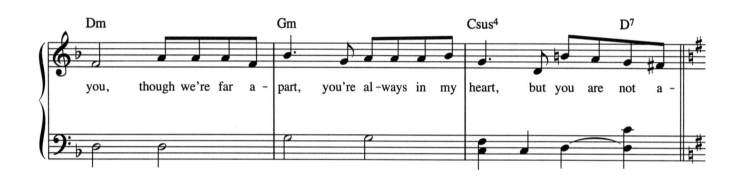

you, though we're far a - part, you're al - ways in my heart, but you are not a -

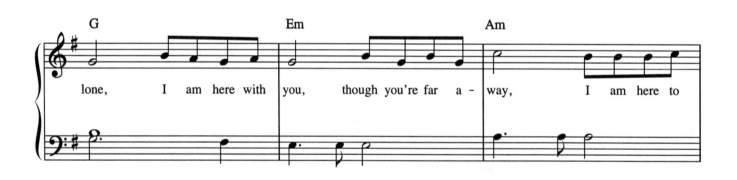

lone, I am here with you, though you're far a - way, I am here to

stay, but you are not a - lone, but I am here with you, though we're far a -

part,   you're al - ways in my   heart,   you are not a - lone.

Repeat ad lib. to fade

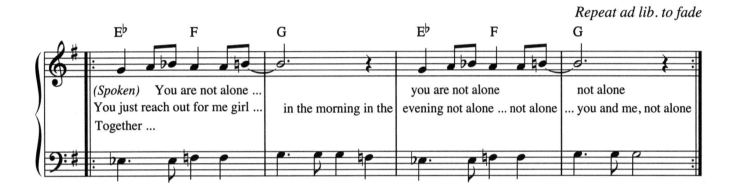

(Spoken)   You are not alone ...   you are not alone   not alone

You just reach out for me girl ... in the morning in the   evening not alone ... not alone   ... you and me, not alone

Together ...

Verse 2:

You are not alone
I am here with you
Though you're far away
I am here to stay.
You are not alone
I am here with you
Though we're far apart
You're aways in my heart.
But you are not alone.

Verse 3:

Just the other night
I thought I heard you cry
Asking me to go
And hold you in my arms.
I can hear your breaths
Your burdens I will bear
But first I need you here
Then forever can begin.

Verse 4:

You are not alone
I am here with you
Though you're far away
I am here to stay.
But you are not alone
But I am here with you
Though we're far apart
You're always in my heart.
But you are not alone.

11/98 (32651)

Each volume is specially arranged by Stephen Duro in extra-easy keys, so that the music fits comfortably to your hands, and includes lyrics (where appropriate) and chord symbols.

Collect the full series...

Abba *Order No. AM91038*
Bach *Order No. AM91041*
Ballads *Order No. AM89944*
Beethoven *Order No. AM91042*
Blues *Order No. AM91507*
Children's Songs *Order No. AM89953*
Richard Clayderman *Order No. AM91501*
Classics *Order No. AM89927*

Simply, the easiest
books of popular music
for piano ever!

Christmas *Order No. AM91509*
Folk Songs *Order No. AM91366*
Handel *Order No. AM91299*
Love Themes *Order No. AM91508*
Marches *Order No. AM91365*
Mozart *Order No. AM91043*
Operatic Arias *Order No. AM91312*
Pops *Order No. AM89939*
Rock 'n' Roll *Order No. AM91040*
Show Tunes *Order No. AM91039*
Symphonic Themes *Order No. AM91313*
Hits of the 50s *Order No. AM91502*
Hits of the 60s *Order No. AM91503*
Hits of the 70s *Order No. AM91504*
Hits of the 80s *Order No. AM91505*
The Beatles *Order No. AM89912*
The Beatles 2 *Order No. NO90571*
The Carpenters *Order No. AM91500*
TV Themes *Order No. AM89968*
Viennese Waltzes *Order No. AM91314*

Available from all good music shops

In case of difficulty, please contact:
Music Sales Limited
Newmarket Road,
Bury St. Edmunds,
Suffolk IP33 3YB, England
Telephone: 0284 702600
Fax: 0284 768301